MW01015809

I'm Expecting!

Yoga Journal Prenatal Edition

Daybook Heaven Books

DAYBOOK HEAVEN

BOOKS

DATE: __Jan 8/19   17 ish weeks   8:30am__

NEXT DOCTORS' APPOINTMENT:

_____

HOW ARE YOU FEELING TODAY?

Mood: __calm__

Energy: __lots__

Appetite: __nothing crazy - not hungry yet__

Morning Sickness? __no__

Cravings? __no__

NOTES

woke up this morning thinking of other
mothers. Some good some resistance/comparing.
Did some breath following. Will do
more now.
   My preggo tea.
      Nettles, red raspberry
      oatstraw
      ginger
      nori flakes
      star anise

Going to start on painting today.

Place
Pictures
Here

Today's Yoga

Before Yoga, I feel...

calm, a bit tight in my back

Today's Practice

Pose	Reps		Total Time
breathe w/ hip circles/waves			
hands and feet series			
gate pose			
down dog			
child pose			
resolved child mantain pose side stretch			
squat side stretch			
warrior			
side stretch warrior			
standing forward fold			
standing bendy circles			1.5 hour

reclined knees open w/ bolster

After Yoga, I feel...

more open upright in my back, hungry

Notes

start with pelvic floor pulses
slow + fast and floor shakes.
side stretches feel the best
also standing in 4th plié with big
spinal/waist rotations.

DATE: _____

NEXT DOCTORS' APPOINTMENT:

_____

HOW ARE YOU FEELING TODAY?

Mood: _____

Energy: _____

Appetite: _____

Morning Sickness? _____

Cravings? _____

NOTES

_____

_____

_____

_____

_____

_____

_____

_____

_____

_____

_____

_____

_____

_____

_____

_____

_____

Place
Pictures
Here

Today's Yoga

Date: ⬭

Before Yoga, I feel...

....

....

Today's Practice

Pose	Reps		Total Time

After Yoga, I feel...

....

....

Notes

....

....

....

....

DATE: _____

NEXT DOCTORS' APPOINTMENT:

_____

HOW ARE YOU FEELING TODAY?

Mood: _____

Energy: _____

Appetite: _____

Morning Sickness? _____

Cravings? _____

NOTES

_____

_____

_____

_____

_____

_____

_____

_____

_____

_____

_____

_____

_____

_____

_____

_____

_____

_____

Place
Pictures
Here

_____

_____

_____

_____

_____

_____

_____

_____

_____

_____

_____

_____

_____

_____

_____

_____

_____

_____

_____

_____

_____

_____

Today's Yoga

Date: ⬭

Before Yoga, I feel...

....

....

Today's Practice

Pose	Reps		Total Time

After Yoga, I feel...

....

....

Notes

....

....

....

....

DATE: _____

NEXT DOCTORS' APPOINTMENT:

_____

HOW ARE YOU FEELING TODAY?

Mood: _____

Energy: _____

Appetite: _____

Morning Sickness? _____

Cravings? _____

NOTES

_____
_____
_____
_____
_____
_____
_____
_____
_____
_____
_____
_____
_____
_____
_____
_____
_____
_____
_____
_____

Place
Pictures
Here

Today's Yoga

Date: ⬭

Before Yoga, I feel...

....

....

Today's Practice

Pose	Reps		Total Time

After Yoga, I feel...

....

....

Notes

....

....

....

....

DATE: _____

NEXT DOCTORS' APPOINTMENT:

_____

HOW ARE YOU FEELING TODAY?

Mood: _____

Energy: _____

Appetite: _____

Morning Sickness? _____

Cravings? _____

NOTES

_____
_____
_____
_____
_____
_____
_____
_____
_____
_____
_____
_____
_____
_____
_____
_____
_____

Place
Pictures
Here

Today's Yoga

Date: ⬭

Before Yoga, I feel...

....

....

Today's Practice

Pose	Reps		Total Time

After Yoga, I feel...

....

....

Notes

....

....

....

....

DATE: _____

NEXT DOCTORS' APPOINTMENT:

_____

HOW ARE YOU FEELING TODAY?

Mood: _____

Energy: _____

Appetite: _____

Morning Sickness? _____

Cravings? _____

NOTES

_____
_____
_____
_____
_____
_____
_____
_____
_____
_____
_____
_____
_____
_____
_____
_____
_____
_____

Place
Pictures
Here

Today's Yoga

Date: ⬭

Before Yoga, I feel...

....

....

Today's Practice

Pose	Reps		Total Time

After Yoga, I feel...

....

....

Notes

....

....

....

....

DATE: _____

NEXT DOCTORS' APPOINTMENT:

_____

HOW ARE YOU FEELING TODAY?

Mood: _____

Energy: _____

Appetite: _____

Morning Sickness? _____

Cravings? _____

NOTES

_____
_____
_____
_____
_____
_____
_____
_____
_____
_____
_____
_____
_____
_____
_____
_____
_____
_____
_____

Place
Pictures
Here

Today's Yoga

Date: ⬭

Before Yoga, I feel...

....

....

Today's Practice

Pose	Reps		Total Time

After Yoga, I feel...

....

....

Notes

....

....

....

....

DATE: _____

NEXT DOCTORS' APPOINTMENT:

_____

HOW ARE YOU FEELING TODAY?

Mood: _____

Energy: _____

Appetite: _____

Morning Sickness? _____

Cravings? _____

NOTES

_____

_____

_____

_____

_____

_____

_____

_____

_____

_____

_____

_____

_____

_____

_____

_____

_____

_____

Place
Pictures
Here

Today's Yoga

Date: ⬭

Before Yoga, I feel...

....

....

Today's Practice

Pose	Reps		Total Time

After Yoga, I feel...

....

....

Notes

....

....

....

....

DATE: _____

NEXT DOCTORS' APPOINTMENT:

_____

HOW ARE YOU FEELING TODAY?

Mood: _____

Energy: _____

Appetite: _____

Morning Sickness? _____

Cravings? _____

NOTES

_____
_____
_____
_____
_____
_____
_____
_____
_____
_____
_____
_____
_____
_____
_____
_____
_____
_____

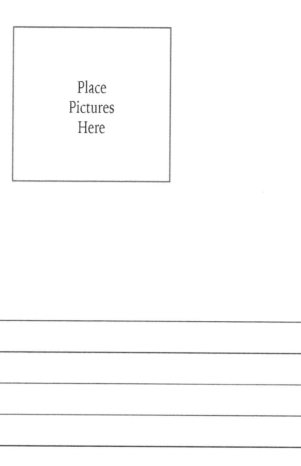

Place
Pictures
Here

Today's Yoga

Date: ☐

Before Yoga, I feel...

....

....

Today's Practice

Pose	Reps		Total Time

After Yoga, I feel...

....

....

Notes

....

....

....

....

DATE: _____

NEXT DOCTORS' APPOINTMENT:

_____

HOW ARE YOU FEELING TODAY?

Mood: _____

Energy: _____

Appetite: _____

Morning Sickness? _____

Cravings? _____

NOTES

_____
_____
_____
_____
_____
_____
_____
_____
_____
_____
_____
_____
_____
_____
_____
_____
_____
_____

Place
Pictures
Here

Today's Yoga

Date: ⬭

Before Yoga, I feel...

....

....

Today's Practice

Pose	Reps		Total Time

After Yoga, I feel...

....

....

Notes

....

....

....

....

DATE: _____

NEXT DOCTORS' APPOINTMENT:

_____

HOW ARE YOU FEELING TODAY?

Mood: _____

Energy: _____

Appetite: _____

Morning Sickness? _____

Cravings? _____

NOTES

_____
_____
_____
_____
_____
_____
_____
_____
_____
_____
_____
_____
_____
_____
_____
_____
_____
_____

Place
Pictures
Here

Today's Yoga

Before Yoga, I feel...

....
....

Today's Practice

Pose	Reps		Total Time

After Yoga, I feel...

....
....

Notes

....
....
....
....

DATE: _____

NEXT DOCTORS' APPOINTMENT:

_____

HOW ARE YOU FEELING TODAY?

Mood: _____

Energy: _____

Appetite: _____

Morning Sickness? _____

Cravings? _____

NOTES

_____
_____
_____
_____
_____
_____
_____
_____
_____
_____
_____
_____
_____
_____
_____
_____
_____
_____
_____
_____
_____

Place
Pictures
Here

Today's Yoga

Date: ⬭

Before Yoga, I feel...

....

....

Today's Practice

Pose	Reps		Total Time

After Yoga, I feel...

....

....

Notes

....

....

....

....

DATE: _____

NEXT DOCTORS' APPOINTMENT:

_____

HOW ARE YOU FEELING TODAY?

Mood: _____

Energy: _____

Appetite: _____

Morning Sickness? _____

Cravings? _____

NOTES

_____
_____
_____
_____
_____
_____
_____
_____
_____
_____
_____
_____
_____
_____
_____
_____
_____
_____

Place
Pictures
Here

Today's Yoga

Before Yoga, I feel...

....

....

Today's Practice

Pose	Reps		Total Time

After Yoga, I feel...

....

....

Notes

....

....

....

....

DATE: _____

NEXT DOCTORS' APPOINTMENT:

_____

HOW ARE YOU FEELING TODAY?

Mood: _____

Energy: _____

Appetite: _____

Morning Sickness? _____

Cravings? _____

NOTES

_____

_____

_____

_____

_____

_____

_____

_____

_____

_____

_____

_____

_____

_____

_____

_____

_____

_____

Place
Pictures
Here

Today's Yoga

Date: _____

Before Yoga, I feel...

....

....

Today's Practice

Pose	Reps		Total Time

After Yoga, I feel...

....

....

Notes

....

....

....

....

DATE: _____

NEXT DOCTORS' APPOINTMENT:

_____

HOW ARE YOU FEELING TODAY?

Mood: _____

Energy: _____

Appetite: _____

Morning Sickness? _____

Cravings? _____

NOTES

_____
_____
_____
_____
_____
_____
_____
_____
_____
_____
_____
_____
_____
_____
_____
_____
_____

Place
Pictures
Here

Today's Yoga

Date: ⬭

Before Yoga, I feel...

....

....

Today's Practice

Pose	Reps		Total Time

After Yoga, I feel...

....

....

Notes

....

....

....

....

DATE: _____

NEXT DOCTORS' APPOINTMENT:

_____

HOW ARE YOU FEELING TODAY?

Mood: _____

Energy: _____

Appetite: _____

Morning Sickness? _____

Cravings? _____

NOTES

_____
_____
_____
_____
_____
_____
_____
_____
_____
_____
_____
_____
_____
_____
_____
_____
_____
_____
_____
_____

Place
Pictures
Here

Today's Yoga

Date: ⬭

Before Yoga, I feel...

....

....

Today's Practice

Pose	Reps		Total Time

After Yoga, I feel...

....

....

Notes

....

....

....

....

DATE: _____

NEXT DOCTORS' APPOINTMENT:

_____

HOW ARE YOU FEELING TODAY?

Mood: _____

Energy: _____

Appetite: _____

Morning Sickness? _____

Cravings? _____

NOTES

_____
_____
_____
_____
_____
_____
_____
_____
_____
_____
_____
_____
_____
_____
_____
_____
_____
_____

Place
Pictures
Here

Today's Yoga

Date: ⬭

Before Yoga, I feel...

....

....

Today's Practice

Pose	Reps		Total Time

After Yoga, I feel...

....

....

Notes

....

....

....

....

DATE: _____

NEXT DOCTORS' APPOINTMENT:

_____

HOW ARE YOU FEELING TODAY?

Mood: _____

Energy: _____

Appetite: _____

Morning Sickness? _____

Cravings? _____

NOTES

_____

_____

_____

_____

_____

_____

_____

_____

_____

_____

_____

_____

_____

_____

_____

_____

_____

_____

_____

_____

Place
Pictures
Here

Today's Yoga

Date:

Before Yoga, I feel...

....

....

Today's Practice

Pose	Reps		Total Time

After Yoga, I feel...

....

....

Notes

....

....

....

....

DATE: _____

NEXT DOCTORS' APPOINTMENT:

_____

HOW ARE YOU FEELING TODAY?

Mood: _____

Energy: _____

Appetite: _____

Morning Sickness? _____

Cravings? _____

NOTES

_____
_____
_____
_____
_____
_____
_____
_____
_____
_____
_____
_____
_____
_____
_____
_____
_____
_____

Place
Pictures
Here

Today's Yoga

Date: ⬭

Before Yoga, I feel...

....

....

Today's Practice

Pose	Reps		Total Time

After Yoga, I feel...

....

....

Notes

....

....

....

....

DATE: _____

NEXT DOCTORS' APPOINTMENT:

_____

HOW ARE YOU FEELING TODAY?

Mood: _____

Energy: _____

Appetite: _____

Morning Sickness? _____

Cravings? _____

NOTES

_____
_____
_____
_____
_____
_____
_____
_____
_____
_____
_____
_____
_____
_____
_____
_____
_____
_____
_____
_____
_____

Place
Pictures
Here

Today's Yoga

Before Yoga, I feel...

....

....

Today's Practice

Pose	Reps		Total Time

After Yoga, I feel...

....

....

Notes

....

....

....

....

DATE: _____

NEXT DOCTORS' APPOINTMENT:

_____

HOW ARE YOU FEELING TODAY?

Mood: _____

Energy: _____

Appetite: _____

Morning Sickness? _____

Cravings? _____

NOTES

_____
_____
_____
_____
_____
_____
_____
_____
_____
_____
_____
_____
_____
_____
_____
_____
_____
_____

Place
Pictures
Here

Today's Yoga

Date: ⬭

Before Yoga, I feel...

....

....

Today's Practice

Pose	Reps		Total Time

After Yoga, I feel...

....

....

Notes

....

....

....

....

DATE: _____

NEXT DOCTORS' APPOINTMENT:

_____

HOW ARE YOU FEELING TODAY?

Mood: _____

Energy: _____

Appetite: _____

Morning Sickness? _____

Cravings? _____

NOTES

_____
_____
_____
_____
_____
_____
_____
_____
_____
_____
_____
_____
_____
_____
_____
_____
_____
_____
_____

Place
Pictures
Here

Today's Yoga

Date: ⬭

Before Yoga, I feel...

....

....

Today's Practice

Pose	Reps		Total Time

After Yoga, I feel...

....

....

Notes

....

....

....

....

DATE: _____

NEXT DOCTORS' APPOINTMENT:

_____

HOW ARE YOU FEELING TODAY?

Mood: _____

Energy: _____

Appetite: _____

Morning Sickness? _____

Cravings? _____

NOTES

_____
_____
_____
_____
_____
_____
_____
_____
_____
_____
_____
_____
_____
_____
_____
_____
_____
_____

Place
Pictures
Here

Today's Yoga

Date: ( )

Before Yoga, I feel...

....

....

Today's Practice

Pose	Reps		Total Time

After Yoga, I feel...

....

....

Notes

....

....

....

....

DATE: _____

NEXT DOCTORS' APPOINTMENT:

_____

HOW ARE YOU FEELING TODAY?

Mood: _____

Energy: _____

Appetite: _____

Morning Sickness? _____

Cravings? _____

NOTES

_____

_____

_____

_____

_____

_____

_____

_____

_____

_____

_____

_____

_____

_____

_____

_____

_____

_____

_____

Place
Pictures
Here

Today's Yoga

Date: ⬭

Before Yoga, I feel...

....

....

Today's Practice

Pose	Reps		Total Time

After Yoga, I feel...

....

....

Notes

....

....

....

....

DATE: _____

NEXT DOCTORS' APPOINTMENT:

_____

HOW ARE YOU FEELING TODAY?

Mood: _____

Energy: _____

Appetite: _____

Morning Sickness? _____

Cravings? _____

NOTES

_____
_____
_____
_____
_____
_____
_____
_____
_____
_____
_____
_____
_____
_____
_____
_____
_____

Place
Pictures
Here

Today's Yoga

Date: ⬭

Before Yoga, I feel...

....

....

Today's Practice

Pose	Reps		Total Time

After Yoga, I feel...

....

....

Notes

....

....

....

....

DATE: _____

NEXT DOCTORS' APPOINTMENT:

_____

HOW ARE YOU FEELING TODAY?

Mood: _____

Energy: _____

Appetite: _____

Morning Sickness? _____

Cravings? _____

NOTES

_____
_____
_____
_____
_____
_____
_____
_____
_____
_____
_____
_____
_____
_____
_____
_____
_____
_____
_____
_____

Place
Pictures
Here

Today's Yoga

Date: ⬭

Before Yoga, I feel...

....

....

Today's Practice

Pose	Reps		Total Time

After Yoga, I feel...

....

....

Notes

....

....

....

....

DATE: _____

NEXT DOCTORS' APPOINTMENT:

_____

HOW ARE YOU FEELING TODAY?

Mood: _____

Energy: _____

Appetite: _____

Morning Sickness? _____

Cravings? _____

NOTES

_____
_____
_____
_____
_____
_____
_____
_____
_____
_____
_____
_____
_____
_____
_____
_____
_____
_____

Place
Pictures
Here

Today's Yoga

Date: ⬭

Before Yoga, I feel...

....
....

Today's Practice

Pose	Reps		Total Time

After Yoga, I feel...

....
....

Notes

....
....
....
....

DATE: _____

NEXT DOCTORS' APPOINTMENT:

_____

HOW ARE YOU FEELING TODAY?

Mood: _____

Energy: _____

Appetite: _____

Morning Sickness? _____

Cravings? _____

NOTES

_____

_____

_____

_____

_____

_____

_____

_____

_____

_____

_____

_____

_____

_____

_____

_____

_____

_____

_____

Place
Pictures
Here

Today's Yoga

Date: ⟨⟩

Before Yoga, I feel...

....

....

Today's Practice

Pose	Reps		Total Time

After Yoga, I feel...

....

....

Notes

....

....

....

....

DATE: _____

NEXT DOCTORS' APPOINTMENT:

_____

HOW ARE YOU FEELING TODAY?

Mood: _____

Energy: _____

Appetite: _____

Morning Sickness? _____

Cravings? _____

NOTES

_____
_____
_____
_____
_____
_____
_____
_____
_____
_____
_____
_____
_____
_____
_____
_____
_____
_____

Place
Pictures
Here

Today's Yoga

Date: ⬭

Before Yoga, I feel...

....

....

Today's Practice

Pose	Reps		Total Time

After Yoga, I feel...

....

....

Notes

....

....

....

....

DATE: _____

NEXT DOCTORS' APPOINTMENT:

_____

HOW ARE YOU FEELING TODAY?

Mood: _____

Energy: _____

Appetite: _____

Morning Sickness? _____

Cravings? _____

NOTES

_____
_____
_____
_____
_____
_____
_____
_____
_____
_____
_____
_____
_____
_____
_____
_____
_____
_____

Place
Pictures
Here

Today's Yoga

Date: ⬭

Before Yoga, I feel...

....

....

Today's Practice

Pose	Reps		Total Time

After Yoga, I feel...

....

....

Notes

....

....

....

....

E: _____

NEXT DOCTORS' APPOINTMENT:

_____

HOW ARE YOU FEELING TODAY?

Mood: _____

Energy: _____

Appetite: _____

Morning Sickness? _____

Cravings? _____

NOTES

_____
_____
_____
_____
_____
_____
_____
_____
_____
_____
_____
_____
_____
_____
_____
_____
_____
_____

Place
Pictures
Here

Today's Yoga

Date: ⬭

Before Yoga, I feel...

....

....

Today's Practice

Pose	Reps		Total Time

After Yoga, I feel...

....

....

Notes

....

....

....

....

DATE: _____

NEXT DOCTORS' APPOINTMENT:

_____

HOW ARE YOU FEELING TODAY?

Mood: _____

Energy: _____

Appetite: _____

Morning Sickness? _____

Cravings? _____

NOTES

_____

_____

_____

_____

_____

_____

_____

_____

_____

_____

_____

_____

_____

_____

_____

_____

_____

_____

Place
Pictures
Here

Today's Yoga

Date:

Before Yoga, I feel...

....

....

Today's Practice

Pose	Reps		Total Time

After Yoga, I feel...

....

....

Notes

....

....

....

....

DATE: _____

NEXT DOCTORS' APPOINTMENT:

_____

HOW ARE YOU FEELING TODAY?

Mood: _____

Energy: _____

Appetite: _____

Morning Sickness? _____

Cravings? _____

NOTES

_____
_____
_____
_____
_____
_____
_____
_____
_____
_____
_____
_____
_____
_____
_____
_____
_____
_____